This above all: To thine own self be true

—WILLIAM SHAKESPEARE

SELF-ESTEEM:
A PRIMER

by
Yehuda Lieberman, LCSW

All identifying information, including name, age, gender, and situation has been changed as appropriate to protect confidentiality. Any similarity to persons, living or dead, is purely coincidental.

ISBN: 0615537677
ISBN 13: 9780615537672
Library of Congress Control Number: 2011938521
Midwood Consulting, Brooklyn, NY

CONTENTS:

INTRODUCTION:
A Psychotherapist's Journey ix

CHAPTER ONE:

Defining Self-Esteem.. 3

CHAPTER TWO:

Early Creation of Sense of Self.................................... 17

CHAPTER THREE:

Environmental Factors 29

CHAPTER FOUR:

The Importance and Impact of Self-Esteem 45

CHAPTER FIVE:

Varying Levels of Self-Esteem...................................... 55

CHAPTER SIX:

Recreating Sense of Self... 65

CHAPTER SEVEN:

Overcoming Obstacles 81

ACKNOWLEDGEMENTS

I would like to express my sincerest gratitude to all those who supported my efforts in the creation of this book. Specifically, I would like to thank my wife for listening to my frequent dissertations on the subject of self-esteem, and for her constant input.

I would like to thank Dr. Stanley Bodner, Dr. David Lefkowitz, Dr. Marc Metzger, and Rabbi Dr. Abraham J. Twerski for reviewing the manuscript and for their critical comments and kind words.

Most importantly, I would like to thank all of my former and current patients who have helped me to understand the meaning of true self-esteem. Without you, this book would never have been possible.

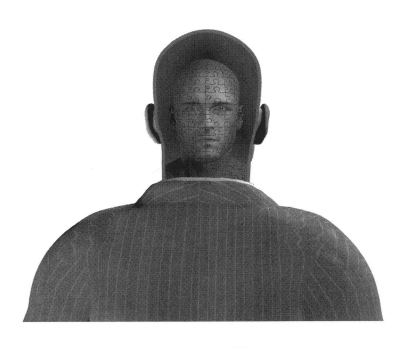

I want you to be everything that's you,
deep at the center of your being.
—*Confucius*

INTRODUCTION

A Psychotherapist's Journey

As a psychotherapist in private practice, I have seen hundreds of people over the years complaining of issues ranging from depression and anxiety to OCD and ADHD. In my training, I studied various forms of therapy, all focused on reducing the symptoms of mental disorders. Some of these therapeutic techniques focus on the symptoms themselves; others place emphasis on the underlying causes. The former typically employ techniques to work directly on specific symptoms and to thus directly reduce their prominence. The latter attempt to identify and resolve the issues that caused the problems in the first place.

When I first began practicing, most of the tools that I employed to help my patients were based on what I had learned in school and under supervision. I used specific techniques to decrease depression, general anxiety, phobias, and other symptoms. My understanding of the causes and bases of these symptoms was somewhat rigid in that I was operating on the theories and assumptions that I had learned throughout my training. In speaking with other mental health professionals, it was clear that clinicians took certain things for granted—for instance, the belief that low self-esteem is a symptom of depression. Then there were things that were considered to be self-explanatory and self-evident, such as what self-esteem is. We took it for granted that we all understood it in the same way.

As time went on, I began to develop my own theories with relation to general symptomatology. I began to realize that some of the commonly held notions about the human mind and its development are seriously lacking. Based on my theories, I developed new tools to help people grow and change. Once these tools were fine-tuned and individually tailored, I saw the effectiveness of treatment radically increase. Patients who had been treated with every imaginable therapeutic technique without improvement were having significant success in reducing their symptoms and often completely changing their lives.

At first, I was simply content with the results of this new treatment method and incorporated it into my practice. However, the more my patients and I explored this new treatment and understood its implications, the more I realized that it is not simply a targeted therapeutic treatment: it has the capacity to completely change our outlook on life, including the way we view ourselves and others. It became increasingly apparent that we could all greatly benefit from this basic change in our way of thinking.

As the power of this fundamental change to our thinking became clear, I began to apply its lessons to my own life. I began changing the way I view myself. This, in turn, helped me identify similarities in the ways that my patients saw themselves.

In writing this book, I did my best to provide as much insight as possible into the many facets and nuances of the process of searching for and attaining true self-esteem. Though the nature of self-esteem can vary between individuals, I tried hard in this book to replicate the process that I use in therapy, which has proven to be effective for greatly increasing self-esteem among people from many different cultures and backgrounds.

Although no work of this sort can be exhaustive, I have endeavored to include as many aspects of the process as possible. The chapters in this book often follow the sequence of my therapy sessions with regard to theory and practice. While conducting sessions with patients, I often found myself identifying important ideas and strategies to add to this book.

I hope this book helps all who read it. The development of the theories and processes of realizing true self-esteem has been quite a journey, both for my patients and for me.

Being is. Being is in-itself.
Being is what it is.
—*Sartre*

CHAPTER ONE
Defining Self-Esteem

What is self-esteem? This seemingly elusive term is often bandied about by professionals and laymen alike. "I have no self-esteem," "You need to build your self-esteem," and "My self-esteem took a hit" have become common phrases. Building self-esteem has, in many ways, become the mantra of modern society. It is spoken of in the school system and among mental health and other professionals. Parents worry about the self-esteem of their children. What, however, do people mean when they speak of self-esteem? Sometimes they are speaking of a sense of one's abilities. Parents, for example, often worry about their children's ability to socialize with their peers and the relationship of this ability to "self-esteem." Many parents tend to view their children's sense of self as clearly linked to a specific ability or activity ("John is an athletic kid"; "Kim is a helpful person"), or to more general ones ("Steve is always there for you"). Notice how John, Kim, and Steve have all been defined based on their actions—the things that others see them doing.

Many adults similarly equate their own sense of self with their sense of importance and capability ("I am a powerful woman"; "I am a senior executive"). Once again, this works as a self-perpetuating association—if they feel important and capable, they feel good about themselves; if they feel good about themselves, they feel important and capable. As long as this association continues in a positive direction, it is sustainable. If, however, the association falters, a negative cycle often begins in which the person feels less important and capable, therefore less good about themselves, and so on.

The senior executive who bases his feelings about himself primarily on *being* a senior executive will take a direct hit to his self-esteem if he gets fired, or even when he retires. Similarly, the woman who only feels good about herself because she is powerful will experience self-esteem issues when her power wanes. In these instances, there is often an unconscious response that works feverishly to replace the original basis of the self-esteem with another. During this period of time, depression and anxiety often result, due both to the initial blow to their perceived sense of self and to this frenetic internal search for a new basis for a sense of self. It is only once a new focus for a sense of self has been developed that the person once again becomes happier and more relaxed.

I have had many patients who have striven for status in their careers, or for achievements in their charitable or other activities, solely for the perceived ability of these roles to make them feel *something* about themselves. These are typically people who have practically no sense of self and are trying, in some way, to create a positive feeling about who they are.

I recall a patient named Sarah, in her late eighties, who sought therapy when she began having panic attacks. She was also deeply depressed for the first time in her life. She couldn't understand how she could fall prey to such conditions, as she had always been an extremely strong person, both physically and emotionally.

As our sessions continued, I noticed that this idea of strength was almost a mantra for Sarah. She constantly reminded me—and herself—of her past strength and importance. It became increasingly obvious that she had always based her sense of self on these factors; she had no sense of self separate from them. And as her strength diminished over time, she came to rely on her memory of them more and more. As this occurred, she became increasingly depressed and anxious.

Having for her entire life defined herself solely as being a strong and capable person, Sarah had no way of knowing the deceptive nature of this sense of self. Nor did she have the tools with which to begin replacing that self-definition with another one.

Aside from the near inevitability of the loss of an externally based sense of self, even those who are able to indefinitely sustain their sense of self on this basis often suffer negative side effects. Because the external aspects of their lives are so crucial to their ability to feel good about themselves, there is a constant anxiety related to maintaining them.

This is often the reason that very wealthy people feel the need to continually accumulate more wealth: it has become the focal point of their self-identity. There is a sense that once a particular goal is reached, that will make them feel good about themselves. Once that goal is achieved, however, the recognition that they do not feel good about themselves causes them to set another goal, then another.

Most people base at least a small portion of their feelings about themselves on things external to them—their job, their relationships, their abilities, and other external forces. There is a wide spectrum of the degree to which we rely on these things to define ourselves. As with most spectrums, a few of us exist at the extreme ends, with most of us falling somewhere in the middle. Within the middle, however, there is much room to move.

To this point, we have not actually defined self-esteem, but have instead discussed many people's understanding of it as related to actions or capabilities. Self-esteem, however, cannot be defined through actions or capabilities. It is very simply a sense of self, or self-definition, and one's feeling about this definition.

People with true self-esteem are those who know who they are internally. They have a clear inner sense of the kind of person they are. This sense is generally based on many attributes, including kind, nice, interesting, funny, smart, and so on. People with true self-esteem feel good about themselves because they appreciate their intrinsic qualities, not their external ones.

The distinction between a false sense of self-esteem and a true one, based on internal feelings, centers around whether one's sense of self is tied to external factors or to a true internal sense of who he is. For instance, if your attribute is "funny," but you only feel humorous in social situations where you can monitor others' responses, you don't feel that "funny" is something that *defines* you. Rather, you feel that "funny" is something that you *do*.

On the other hand, someone who recognizes that he is intrinsically a funny person can sense this attribute within himself. Without relating "funny" to other people or to specific situations, he simply *feels* funny. That is, he recognizes aspects of himself—his thoughts and feelings—that are humorous.

Someone who has a sense of self that is based on intrinsic attributes does not generally need to base his sense of self on external factors, whether they are people, situations, abilities, or other such externalities. He simply feels good about himself without the need to identify specific externalities.

Many people confuse self-confidence with self-esteem. The reason for this is that the popular notion of self-esteem is of someone who has confidence in himself (i.e., in his *abilities*). A sense of self based on externalities, such as abilities, is not indicative of true self-esteem. Thus self-confidence is a false form of self-esteem because it speaks to people's abilities rather than to their internal attributes. As such, many people that we stereotypically view as having high self-esteem might, in fact, have quite low levels of true self-esteem.

In my psychotherapy practice, I often ask people to define themselves. In most instances, I find that they have some difficulty in doing so. When asked to complete the sentence: "I am a _____ person," the most common response seems to be: "Hmm, well...a good person?" When asked to be more specific, however, many people have trouble coming up with more than one or two attributes to describe themselves. In fact, some people cannot think of even one. Many people have trouble simply contemplating the concept of who they are as being separate from what they do.

Nonetheless, when I follow up on this question by asking the same people to answer the same question with reference to someone they know, they are typically able to name more attributes for their friends or family members than for themselves. This is an indication that the issue is not related to their cognitive ability (or lack thereof) to define inherent traits, but rather to their ability to recognize these qualities in themselves, and therefore to develop a sense of self based on these qualities.

It may be quite easy for me to say, "Robyn is a caring person," almost as an instinctive reaction. It requires little or no thought and is simply the way in which I see Robyn. When it comes to myself, however, it is much more difficult for me to "simply" see myself as something entirely separate from how others see me, what I do, my job title, or other external attributes.

The irony is that though we are naturally egocentric in that we tend to regard ourselves as the center of all things, we nonetheless have trouble separating our beliefs, thoughts, and ideas from those of others. The famous German philosopher, Martin Heidegger, spoke of an existential awareness of self with reference to the definition of "being." The paradox is the juxtaposition of our self-centeredness and our tendency not to be especially self-aware.

Even people who appear to have high self-confidence often have trouble identifying specific personal attributes. Particular reasons for this vary. Parental pressure and emphasis during childhood often play an important role. If a child develops a sense of self based on external factors reinforced by his parents, it becomes very difficult to acknowledge intrinsic attributes later on in life.

Peer pressure often affects a person's basis for his sense of self. Similarly, a person's community and the emphasis placed on specific deeds, appearance, features, and traits can affect his basis for sense of self. A person's need to fit in very often goes hand in hand with his feelings about himself.

Once an intrinsic attribute is identified, the next question that I often ask is, "Without relying on external factors like abilities and your perception of others' views of you, how do you know that you have that particular attribute?" This is a question that is often extremely difficult for people to answer. Having focused their energy for so long on their externally based "sense of self," they have trouble responding to the question without resorting to those external traits.

The best response that I ever received to this question was by a young man who was readily able to recognize the distinction between his internal sense of self and that based on externalities. In response to the question

"What makes you a kind person?" his response was, "I just am."

The point, of course, is that true internalized self-esteem requires no analysis of facts or reference to external characteristics or traits. All that it requires is introspection, leading to the recognition of our personal attributes.

Having defined "true" self-esteem, we can begin to recognize that a scant few of us actually have it. So many of us have never even conceptualized self-esteem in this manner; instead, we have bought into the notion that self-esteem is based on things external to us. We have trouble accepting the idea that it is based on nothing other than our innate sense of self, and the fact that most of us do not have this innate sense of self points to the fact that low self-esteem appears to have reached epidemic proportions.

What we achieve inwardly will change outer reality.
— Lucius Mestrius Plutarchus (Plutarch)

CHAPTER TWO

Early Creation of Sense of Self

How does self-esteem develop? What causes some of us to assume a sense of self that is based on external factors, thus inhibiting us from developing true self-esteem, while others are seemingly able to naturally develop an intrinsic sense of self?

There is a basic need for people to have a sense of self. Without any sense of who we are, we tend to feel unimportant and worthless, and life can appear pointless. It is this basic need that causes most people to automatically develop a sense of self. While some of us are able to feel positively toward ourselves based on our internal thoughts and feelings, many are unable to do so. These people, by default, base their feelings and thoughts about themselves on externalities.

The reasons that people look outside of themselves to establish a sense of self are complicated and highly individualized, in that there is no single factor that can explain the cause of low self-esteem in most people. Whatever the initial cause, as time goes on it becomes increasingly difficult for a person to base his sense of self on anything other than what he has become accustomed to; in fact, without conscious effort, it appears to be nearly impossible to do.

A patient of mine named David illustrates this point. David was raised by parents with a particularly turbulent marriage. From a young age, he learned that he could often alleviate the tension within the family by taking charge. Although he had older siblings, he was the one who developed this ability. He asserted himself as the caretaker—making decisions, forging alliances, and establishing compromises.

As David grew older, his caretaking role in the family became more pronounced as his responsibilities grew. The family relied increasingly heavily on his leadership and caretaking, and by the time he was a teenager, the family consulted him about all family issues. David became the primary decision-maker in the family. As an adult, the family did nothing without David's agreement and approval, even long after he had moved out of his childhood home and was married with children.

Over the years, as David's status in the family formed solidly into that of controller and caretaker, he naturally viewed himself increasingly in this way as well. As he grew up, his sense of self, initially formed through perceived necessity and specific to the family situation, became increasingly internalized and generalized. Even once he was removed from the nuclear family (having married and begun his own family) and that role was no longer necessary, he was nonetheless unable to view himself in any other way. He was unable to conceive of himself as having any attributes other than "being in control" or "caretaking."

In every aspect of his life, David experienced a need to be in control. If anything was out of sync—even something simple like the orderliness of a room—he felt compelled to fix it. If he forced himself to ignore it, he would become highly anxious. Not only did he need to be in control of issues that arose, but he always needed to have an active issue—thus, if no issues presented themselves, he unconsciously created one. This led to anxiety and the inability to relax and enjoy anything.

In therapy, David was able to recognize that his need to control everything in his life was directly due to his need to define himself. Having always defined himself by his ability to control, he was unable to feel *anything* about himself unless he was controlling something. It was difficult for David even to recognize his need to control as the basis for his sense of self. Once he *had* become cognizant of this, it was even more difficult for him to contemplate, even from a purely cognitive perspective, his feelings toward himself as based on anything else. As far as he was concerned, this was who he was.

Over time, David learned to acknowledge both his need to control and the origins of this need. As he learned to focus on his intrinsic qualities, he slowly began relinquishing his need for control. As his need for control diminished, his anxiety diminished as well.

I had another patient named Gloria who sought therapy due to her increasingly problematic bouts of depression. In therapy, it became clear that these feelings presented themselves when she was forced to think about the kind of person that she was. When someone asked her a question or made a comment pertaining to her sense of who she was, she described feeling empty and "hazy."

Gloria began to recognize that she often unconsciously mimicked the personalities and behavior of others around her. She would feel the way that she perceived that they felt. She caught herself adopting their mannerisms and would sometimes even pick up their foreign accents in speaking with them.

Having been raised in a culture that did not recognize women's rights, Gloria grew up with the sense that her thoughts and feelings were unimportant, which in turn contributed to her general lack of a sense of self. The sense that she had no inherent worth forced Gloria to latch onto anything external that offered some sense of identity. This included her unconscious assumption of the mannerisms of other people, as she mirrored what she perceived to be the other's "self." Her acknowledgement of her tendency to do this, and her subsequent recognition of the reasons for it was the first step in Gloria's development of her own internal sense of self.

As these examples illustrate, the development of a sense of self begins in childhood. Many factors and issues contribute to this development. A common practice in parenting that encourages children to look externally for their sense of identity is to place emphasis on the child rather than on the child's action. How often have we heard, or said, the phrase, "Bad boy!" or "Bad girl!", when what might otherwise have been said is, "You did a bad thing." Placing the emphasis on the child tells them that their actions make them who they are. The message is that this particular action makes the child "bad," at least for a period of time, whereas saying "You did a bad thing" lets him know that his essence doesn't change as a result of his actions.

Aside from this immediate impact, children who are often told that they are bad can become unable to distinguish generally between what they do and who they are. This makes it almost inevitable that, as they grow up, their sense of self will become based on their actions, and then on other external factors. If these types of statements are often repeated, constantly sending the message to the child that his actions make him bad, he will begin to accept his conception of "bad" as his sense of self. Once this occurs, in order to retain this sense of self, the child needs to continue doing bad things. This becomes a vicious cycle, whereby the constructed sense of self causes inappropriate behavior, which in turn reinforces the negative sense of self.

Erik Erikson was an eminent psychoanalyst known for his theory on social development. The fifth stage in his theory of psychosocial development is "Identity vs. Role Confusion." This developmental crisis speaks to an adolescent's new concern with how he feels about himself. The beginning of this stage (about age 13-14) generally coincides with the beginning of high school. According to Erikson, this is the time in an adolescent's life when he begins to develop his sense of self.

As with all of Erikson's stages, the emphasis is largely placed on how the person passes through the crisis with reference to the external world. In fact, the very title of the stage, "Identity vs. Role Confusion," speaks to the person's ability to develop an identity based on his roles. According to the theory, in successfully passing through a particular stage the person develops a certain sense about himself. By the time a person completes high school, this psychosocial stage is almost over (it ends at about age 19-20). According to Erikson, it is at this point that a person should have a clear "sense of self." Erikson's theory makes one general assumption—the same assumption made by most of us: he assumes that a sense of self needs to be based on the external world, and therefore on our thoughts, feelings, ideas, abilities and general interaction, specifically with reference to factors external to us. (It is for this reason that he places the stage of identity creation at a point when roles are typically established) (1950).

Abraham Maslow's theory of the "Hierarchy of Needs," on the other hand, *does* refer to an internalized sense of self. His fifth and final stage in his theory of the Hierarchy of Needs is that of "self-actualization," which refers to the realization of personal potential, self-fulfillment and personal growth: "Intrinsic growth of what is already in the organism [i.e., the person], or more accurately of what is the organism itself...self-actualization is growth-motivated rather than deficiency-motivated." (*Psychological Review*, 1949).

However, Maslow's theory is pyramidal in nature. He contends that one cannot begin working on any stage before the previous stages have been successfully completed. As such, before anyone can even begin working on an intrinsic sense of self, as it relates to Maslow's theory of self-actualization, he would need to complete the previous four stages ("Biological and Physiological needs," then "Safety needs," then "Belongingness and Love needs," then, finally, "Esteem needs"). These four stages all focus on externalities such as food and shelter, security, relationships, and achievement. It is therefore

Maslow's contention that we need to successfully satisfy all of these requirements before we can begin to work on our "true" sense of self.

Maslow clearly felt that his understanding of self-actualization was not complete. As such, his conception of how to achieve it was likely lacking, as he himself acknowledged: "Since, in our society, basically satisfied people are the exception, we do not know much about self-actualization, either experimentally or clinically. It remains a challenging problem for research." (*Psychological Review*, 1943).

The focus on external factors with reference to how we view people in society dates back well before the twentieth century. Since at least Aristotle's time, philosophers, in one form or another, have debated the question of egoism versus altruism. This basically refers to the difference between concern for oneself and concern for others. Nonetheless, even this latter, lofty concept is mostly debated with reference to people's actions, the focus placed on actions as defining the person. In order to begin focusing on intrinsic sense of self, we need to completely change a way of thinking that dates back many millennia.

Insanity in individuals is something rare—but in groups, parties, nations and epochs, it is the rule.
—Nietzsche

CHAPTER THREE

Environmental Factors

In chapter 2, we discussed Erik Erikson's stage of Identity vs. Role Confusion. For the moment, let's accept Erikson's contention that the development of identity begins at a time when most people are beginning high school and ends shortly after most people have finished high school. If this is so, the vast majority of our identity development is based around thoughts and feelings that occur within the high school milieu.

We all know that high school can make for a very competitive atmosphere. Cliques tend to form, and adolescents often begin to define themselves based on their frames of reference within these cliques. Jocks see themselves only as jocks; "brainiacs" view themselves only as smart; cool kids recognize in themselves nothing but their popularity among their peers.

If the development of identity does end shortly after high school, those of us who learned to base our sense of self solely on external factors would appear to be stuck with that conceptualization of ourselves. Indeed, we often see people who clearly view themselves very similarly to the way they viewed themselves in high school and whose seemingly adolescent frames of reference are maintained throughout adulthood. This type of adolescent identity can manifest itself in many ways, including intelligent, popular, and athletic, and may persist long after the source of the identification is gone. For example, someone may view himself as a jock, although he's been out of high school for twenty years and has not been on a sports team since that time.

I recall a patient named Joe who came to my office for a consultation, presenting with symptoms of anxiety. When I asked him about his feelings toward high school, he stated unequivocally that high school was the best experience of his life. He was the star center on the school's basketball team. He always had his choice of girlfriends. Everybody looked up to him. He was always surrounded by friends and teammates. Basically his entire social life—and sense of self—was based around his status as a high school basketball player.

When Joe entered college, he was on the college basketball team as well. This continued to reinforce his artificial sense of self. It was only after college that Joe had to close the book on being a jock as he entered the workplace.

In the corporate world, Joe did well. Over time, however, he began feeling anxious. Having nothing specific that was problematic in his life, Joe couldn't understand the cause of his feelings. Once he began to acknowledge that his entire sense of self was based on one external factor that no longer existed, he was able to recognize his need to create a more internalized sense of self.

People can base their sense of self on various external aspects of their lives: their jobs, physical capabilities, gender, religion, race, ethnicity, or others. What these all have in common, in addition to being external to the individual, is the focus on one aspect as the dominant basis for what they feel about themselves.

Sometimes this value is reinforced in early childhood, often by parents. Children who are constantly told that they are smart often have trouble differentiating between *being* smart (i.e., as an intrinsic sense of who they are) and doing smart things, like getting good grades. As discussed in chapter 2, parents often—intentionally or not—link their children's actions to who they are, so the child learns that he is smart only because he gets good grades; that he is funny only because he gets laughs; or that he is kind only because he does nice things.

Religion and community can also play a strong role in identity formation. People often form a strong sense of belonging with reference to a particular culture or way of life. While this can be a healthy part of one's social life, if it is the sole foundation of one's sense of self, it can be problematic.

Many people view their religion as a part of who they are. This, in and of itself, is not necessarily a problem. When people tell me, for instance, "Jewish is who I am," it basically comes down to semantics. Certainly, being Jewish may be who they are, just as being white, tall, fat, or for that matter human, is who they are. However, these are all descriptions, as opposed to recognition of something about themselves that is intrinsic to them. Though many people would say their religion is part of who they are internally, they are typically referring to their religious faith—their feelings and beliefs—rather than an inherent "Jewishness."

If a person recognizes himself as Jewish in a descriptive context but also clearly recognizes intrinsic aspects of himself, there need be no contradiction between the two. The former is descriptive, while the latter is intrinsic. If, however, his entire sense of self is based around this descriptive facet of his life, his feelings about himself become externalized.

Many people who have no internal sense of worth hide in a group identity. People who develop this sense of group identity in lieu of an individual sense of self often get caught up in the need to be a part of the group. If their identity is solely defined by the group, they need to continually reinforce that sense of belonging, in a manner similar to the reinforcement of any other external sense of self. Peer pressure comes into play, essentially forcing the person to adapt to the ideas and beliefs of the group for fear of losing his sense of identity.

I have been told by many people that they disagree with many of the beliefs and practices of the group to which they belong. Furthermore, acting differently from the other members of the group would have little or no impact on their status within the group. Nonetheless, they feel incapable of changing their patterns of behavior. When they do, they feel high levels of anxiety that only abate when they once again conform to the group. Their anxiety is not due to any external threat (e.g., being ostracized). Rather, it is due to their sense of self being placed under their own scrutiny.

In other groups, the group mentality is so self-definitive that the members of the group feel threatened by any deviation from the group's rituals. These groups tend to be excessively rigid in terms of their design and their belief systems. If a member of the group attempts to act in a way that is contrary to its rigid structure, the identity of the group—and therefore of the individuals in the group—is threatened. This often results in the shunning of the offending member, often leading to his departure from the group. Once this occurs, the group identity seems once again safe. People who are searching for their sense of self often gravitate to this type of group in order to achieve a sense of group identity in the absence of an individual one.

For this reason, people who have no sense of self are particularly vulnerable to the enticement of cults. This is the reason that cults do much of their recruiting on college campuses. College students are often still struggling with the sudden loss of their externally based sense of identity that was developed in high school. This can wreak emotional havoc with their feelings about themselves. Cults appear to offer a new sense of self—one of group identity. This can seem like a lifeline to a young person, perhaps depressed and anxious, struggling to replace his sense of identity.

Once someone begins using a cult, religion, ethnicity, community, belief, or any group to foster his sense of self, it tends to result in a vicious cycle. If the initial impetus was an empty feeling, prompting a search for self-meaning, joining the group can lead to powerful emotions that accompany having finally discovered a sense of self. As time goes on, however, this feeling can mimic the effects of a drug, requiring stronger and more frequent doses by way of adherence to the group dynamic. As this occurs, the person consistently loses more and more of his ability to develop an internal sense of self, resulting in an even greater need to adhere to the group.

This is the reason that cults, and indeed many other forms of group mentality, can be so seductive and so difficult to give up. Many people who have been caught up in cults have come to realize the folly of their ways and the problems inherent in the cult. However, even recognizing the insidious nature of the cult and wanting to leave, they often have trouble doing so. They are caught between their conscious, logical recognition of what is right and their unconscious need to belong in order to feel something about themselves.

Generally, the more exclusive the group, the greater the risk that it will be used in place of true self-esteem. Very closed groups, whether religious, social, industry-specific (i.e., in the Hollywood community), or other exclusive milieu, are particularly prone to this danger, as these groups are often formed specifically for and by people who are searching for a sense of self. Membership in these groups thus becomes contingent on the person's lack of self-esteem.

A central requirement for these groups is that they remain exclusive in that members view themselves as better or different from those not within the group. If people with true self-esteem were to join the group, this would endanger the entire purpose of the group, causing those who still require exclusivity as a basis for sense of self to abandon the group in search of one that would better serve their needs. While the original group might still exist in name, it would no longer serve the purpose for which it was initially created. It would then become a "healthy" group, often no longer having a strong need for exclusivity.

Since the very basis of an unhealthy group is related to its exclusivity, people who belong to these groups to gain a sense of self often develop feelings of antipathy toward those who do not belong to the group. Someone whose sense of self is group-based might begin feeling that the group's demographics, nature, and/or belief system are good and right, in contrast to the characteristics of all other groups. This is likely why bigotry is often found among people who feel a strong attachment to the group to which they belong. For this reason, increasing intrinsic self-esteem often seems to significantly reduce prejudice and racism.

Many of the externalities that form the bases of self-esteem are seductive. We understand why someone would want an identity based on good looks, accomplishments, intelligence, abilities, or membership in a group. These are things that make us feel good about ourselves. The fact that they are all culturally based (in that their importance is dictated to us by the people around us) does not mitigate the intensity of the appeal; it might actually enhance it.

Though most external sense of self is based on seemingly positive ideas, people sometimes develop a sense of self that is clearly based on negative concepts. There are people whose sense of identity has developed around being overweight, sad, isolated, angry, or even being a "bad" person, as discussed in chapter 2.

Although it seems obvious that we would rather have a sense of self based on something positive than to have no sense of self at all, we instinctively seek to form a sense of self regardless of the basis. If positive factors are elusive, a person will often use negative factors to build a sense of self. Though this may seem counterintuitive, people would rather have a negative sense of self than none at all.

We have all known children (and indeed some adults) who constantly do bad things, seemingly for no reason. Very often, they are looking for attention. You might ask why they don't simply do good things to earn attention. Very often, parents and teachers do not recognize the need for children to receive positive reinforcement. When children do well, they are often ignored, either because the positive behavior is not noticed or because it is expected. It is when children misbehave that parents "lavish" them with attention, shouting or otherwise punishing them.

As time goes on, a child can unconsciously acknowledge that he gets more attention when he does negative things than when he does positive ones. This leads him to do more negative things to trigger the attention he craves. This is the point when many parents make the mistake of labeling the child as "bad," often using phrases like "Bad boy!" and "What's the matter with you?" Not only does this promote a pattern of negative behavior, but it also teaches the child that "negative" or "bad" is who they are.

Once a child begins to believe that his identity is solely based on negative features, this is reinforced, both through continued negative comments and through his own continued negative behavior. He begins to believe that he does bad things because he is a bad person, failing to recognize that the real cause of his negative actions is the need for attention and, at a deeper level, for an internally based sense of self. Thus, ironically, the very need to feel good about oneself is often the catalyst for the development of a negative sense of self.

Regardless of a person's basis for his sense of self, recognition of this basis and understanding of the factors that formed it is crucial in order to begin creating a true sense of self based on his internal attributes.

Happiness is the meaning and the purpose of life, the whole aim and end of human existence.
—Aristotle

CHAPTER FOUR

The Importance and Impact of
Self-Esteem

Now that we have defined self-esteem and identified its early development, we need to address the importance of having positive self-esteem. What are the benefits of having true self-esteem, and what are the consequences of having little or no internally based sense of self?

While there are typically a variety of factors inherent in mental health issues, many of which can be strongly impacted by low self-esteem, we will focus specifically on the impact of self-esteem on a few mental health disorders.

In the Diagnostic and Statistical Manual of Mental Disorders (DSM-IV-TR), low self-esteem is listed as a symptom of dysthymic disorder (commonly referred to as dysthymia), a general depressive disorder. Thus, the conventional wisdom of the mental health profession suggests that when someone develops dysthymia, his self-esteem takes a hit.

The problem with this perspective is twofold. Firstly, no one appears to be defining self-esteem. If self-esteem is not clearly defined, how does one know whether his has been lowered? Secondly, since the DSM-IV-TR refers to a person's *current* level of self-esteem with reference to diagnosis, the insinuation is that the "self-esteem" it is referring to is not static, but rather subject to change. If clinicians and laypeople alike have been defining self-esteem as a feeling about oneself that is subject to fluctuations in mood, situation, or surroundings, it is not self-esteem to which they are referring. Self-esteem, by definition, is not subject to change based on external factors. What they appear to be discussing is what I would term "self-image." This would naturally be rather low when a person is depressed.

A question arises: Do feelings of depression cause low self-image (as is suggested) or does low self-image cause feelings of depression?

It seems clear that if a person had a negative self-image, he would begin to feel badly about himself. If this persisted to the point where the person could no longer boost his self-image via external factors, the person would be at risk of becoming depressed. Therefore, it may not be the case that dysthymic disorder causes low "self-esteem," but rather it may be that low "self-esteem" can cause the dysthymia.

If low self-image can cause depression, the obvious assumption would be that in order to reduce feelings of depression one should work on boosting his self-image. Because the common conception of self-image is based on external factors, it would be natural to conclude that boosting one's *external* sense of self would be part of the solution to depression.

Although this might work to some extent in the short-term, it unfortunately only reinforces the initial problem by continuing to focus on self-image as opposed to self-esteem. In the long run, it is very likely that the person would repeatedly succumb to bouts of depression. This often leads to one of two scenarios:

a) The person begins taking medication for depression, leading to long-term dependence or constant changes and termination then restarting of the medication regimen; or

b) After a time, the person no longer feels depressed, but begins to experience other symptoms, like anxiety, anger, and emotional numbness.

In addition to depression, anxiety is another common symptom of low self-esteem. There are many types of anxiety disorders, including acute stress disorder, generalized anxiety disorder (GAD), obsessive-compulsive disorder (OCD), panic disorder (with or without agoraphobia), phobias (including social phobia), and post-traumatic stress disorder (PTSD). What these all have in common is a fear of something often not clearly defined.

A person with an anxiety disorder usually fits into one of two categories. He might be unable to identify the cause of his fear, leaving him not only anxious but also confused and frustrated. Alternatively he might identify a cause for the fear, but recognize that his fear is much greater than is warranted by the source.

People with anxiety will often grasp anything to explain their fears. This helps them to "make sense" of the anxiety and to avoid the confused frustration associated with the inability to identify any reason for the fear. For instance, someone whose job is not going well might assume that his anxiety is related to this, ignoring the fact that his job wasn't going any better for some time before he began feeling anxious. He could also be ignoring the fact that the level of anxiety is disproportionate to his job issues.

Although the physical problem is not the true cause of the anxiety, it can be related to it. In the instance where someone closely defines himself as based on his job (i.e., "I am a brilliant doctor," or "I'm a powerful CEO"), problems related to his job can have a profound impact on his self-image. This can cause high anxiety, not because of the specific job issue, but because his self-image has been assaulted and he has no internal sense of self on which to rely. This often makes it difficult for the person to recognize his fears as reflecting an anxiety disorder. It also makes it more difficult for him to work on the root cause of his anxiety.

I have found that a common component of anxiety (i.e., fear with little or no basis in reality) is low self-esteem. People who have always based their feelings about themselves on externalities, only to have them threatened, often experience a feeling of anxiety. It is at this point that they begin questioning their feelings about their actions, abilities, and other external factors of their self-image. It is only when it becomes obvious that any "apparent" causes (i.e., trouble at work or in a relationship) cannot explain the intensity of their fear that they begin to recognize the need to work on the deeper causes of their anxiety.

Although a person might recognize the need to work on the underlying issues contributing to his anxiety, it is usually very difficult to figure out where to begin. Simply the understanding that there are unconscious issues at work does not necessarily help the person to identify those issues. And even once one is aware of the issues and their impact, it is extremely difficult to know where to begin in treating them.

In most cases, the first step is to clearly recognize that the anxiety is in fact due to an underlying issue rather than the "logical" source to which it is being causally linked (e.g., job problems). Once the person recognizes the unconscious nature of the problem, the next step is to grasp the true meaning of sense of self. At that point, the person is finally able to begin working directly on his self-esteem.

I have included a useful litmus test to determine whether a feeling is appropriate within a given situation or if there appears to be an underlying factor impacting it. The first part is simply to rate the level of the problem on a scale of one to one hundred, then rate the level of anxiety. If there is a clear discrepancy between the two ratings, there may be underlying issues. If, for instance, a person rates her problems on the job at thirty, and her anxiety rates a seventy-five, it is clear that there is something causing the anxiety other than simply the work problems themselves.

The second part of the test relates to the fundamental principle of self-esteem and focuses on a question that is common when discussing sense of self: How do I know whether an external factor is a part of my self-esteem or if it is simply something that I enjoy? What's wrong with loving my job, my abilities, and my belongings?

The simple answer lies in the difference between "want" and "need." If you can clearly recognize that the factor is purely something you want, then it is probably a healthy desire. If, on the other hand, it is something that you require, it is probably essential to your externally based sense of self. This need is what leads to the discrepancy between the level of the actual problem and the level of the anxiety.

When someone *wants* something, its loss can cause feelings ranging from acceptance to consternation. When someone *needs* something, on the other hand, its loss can have devastating and profound consequences.

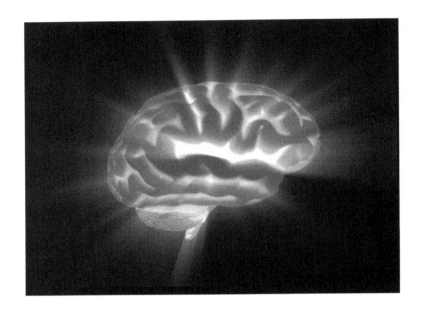

He who is unable to live in society, or who has no need because he is sufficient for himself, must be either a beast or a god.
—Aristotle

CHAPTER FIVE
Varying Levels of Self-Esteem

I have often been asked what the "appropriate" amount of self-esteem is. Is the goal to need nothing? Should we base none of our sense of self and happiness on external values, but base it solely on our feelings about ourselves? If we do, does that negate any sense of accomplishment or drive? Will it make us lose sight of the things that we enjoy?

No two people are alike with regard to both their interest in increasing their sense of self and their ability to accomplish this goal. Some people are content to reach the point where they can generally feel good about themselves, but where they still want to connect a portion of their sense of self to their accomplishments and other external aspects of life. While this may not be optimal from a purist perspective—working to develop a "perfect" sense of self—once someone is clearly cognizant of the true meaning of self-esteem, he is the only one who can make the decision as to his goals.

Other people strive to completely obliterate any and all ties between externality and their sense of self. Their goal is to develop a sense of self that is completely based on internal self-perception. They want to reach the point where none of their looks, possessions, or accomplishments, nor any other external factor can affect their feelings about themselves in any way.

That being said, it would be extremely difficult for anyone to reach that level of self-esteem, and it is highly unlikely that anyone could do so. This would require an intense and dramatic change in the person's way of thinking and feeling to the point where their entire sense of how they view the world has been essentially dismantled and rebuilt.

I recall a patient named Saul who felt that he had reached this level of self-esteem. He had initially sought counseling because he was so obsessed with what others thought that his entire being was focused on this. He worried constantly about what others thought of him.

At first Saul had a tremendous amount of difficulty simply understanding the concept of sense of self. He couldn't wrap his head around the idea that you are not what others think of you. Week after week, he stated with conviction that who you are is based only on what others think of you. Although we focused on other forms of therapy for many months, the concepts of self-esteem and self-perception were always underlying central themes. It took months for Saul to fully comprehend the notion of self-esteem and how it could apply to him.

A short while later, Saul advised me that he had reached the zenith of self-esteem; he had become nasty and uncaring toward others because he no longer required their positive thoughts in order to feel good about himself. I pointed out to him that as long as others are affecting his feelings about himself in any sense, his self-esteem was not entirely internally based. In his case, Saul had replaced his need to feel good as based on others' positive thoughts about him with a need to *not* care about what others thought of him. Although he had felt that he had reached the point where he no longer based his sense of self on others, he had in fact simply created a "reaction formation" where, in order to avoid an unwanted thought, he had created an opposite thought to replace it.

It took a while for Saul to find his happy medium where he was aware of his need for others to feel good about him, but where this was not the sole, or indeed the main, process through which he felt good about himself.

Diogenes of Sinope, the Greek cynic philosopher who lived in the fourth century BCE, lived in a *pithos* (a barrel or tub belonging to the temple of Cybele) to show his contempt for things of the world. He sought to teach by living example that wisdom and happiness belong to the man who is independent of society. Though his point may be well taken, Plato once described Diogenes as "a Socrates gone mad," perhaps because Diogenes could have lived any life that he chose, and he chose the one he did. Put another way, he could have lived in any way that he *wanted* to; however, he may have chosen the life that he did because he felt that he *needed* to do so in order to feel better about himself. Had he enjoyed true self-esteem, he wouldn't have needed to live in a pithos. Like Saul, Diogenes probably defined himself, one way or another, through an externality—in his case by living in the pithos.

In reality, it is highly unlikely that anyone could entirely eliminate his externally based sense of self. Theoretically, however, if a person were to do this, he would be able to completely isolate his needs from his wants, relinquishing the former and focusing on the latter. He would be able to do the things that he wants to do simply because he enjoys them. He would strive to accomplish his goals in order to enjoy a sense of accomplishment, rather than to feel good about himself. He would want to look nice in order to enjoy his looks, not to feel good about others' feelings about him. And he would acquire possessions in order to enjoy them, rather than to "keep up with the Joneses" in order to feel better about who he is.

A person who could accomplish this would enjoy the external aspects of life because he wants them. Then, if he was to lose them, he might be saddened or upset about the loss, but would not feel badly about himself because of an unconscious need to have these things.

Though achieving self-esteem completely free from externalities is likely impossible, we can continually endeavor to move ever closer to this point. Therefore the goal is to strive for an internal sense of self that allows us to feel good about ourselves, while fulfilling our wants (rather than our needs) through external factors.

Regardless of whether the catalysts for our actions are based on need or on want, the underlying motivation is generally happiness. If we analyze our wants and needs, we find that they all stem from our innate yearning to be happy and content.

Someone might want to be successful in order to make money. He wants the money so that he can buy a nice car and a big house, and have money in the bank. These things might make him feel that he is worthwhile or that he is a part of something. Or they might simply help him to be less stressed. Either way, the underlying motivation is the expectation that these things will lead to happiness.

Very often, however, we lose sight of the underlying goal, focusing instead on the process. Instead of recognizing that our goal is to become happier regardless of the way in which it is achieved, we place all of the emphasis on the process. We don't see the forest for the trees. This tends to sabotage our ability to achieve happiness.

If we can learn to adjust our viewpoint and begin to focus on the root goal of becoming happy, we can begin to work directly toward this goal, and see the process for what it is.

Be as you wish to seem.
—*Socrates*

CHAPTER SIX
Recreating Sense of Self

By this point, we have recognized the need to increase self-esteem, and we have also begun to develop the concept that who we are is more than what we do or what others think of us. The next step is to understand how we *should*, in fact, view ourselves, and how to begin recognizing and focusing on our internal sense of self.

I have often been asked how I could say that what we do does not make us who we are. The things that we do indicate to others what types of people we are. In fact, the only way that we can recognize the character of others is through their actions. Furthermore, if what we do does not tell us who we are, then how *do* we know who we are?

Firstly, though we assume things about others based on their actions, this is only by default. We cannot possibly gain access to another's thoughts and feelings, so we have no way of knowing the true reasons for their actions. There are people who do kind things even though they are not kind at heart. And there are those who do not do kind things although they are intrinsically kind. In the former instance, a person might show kindness in order to be thought of in a certain way or because doing nice things was simply ingrained in him as a habit. In the latter instance, a person who is painfully shy might have quite a bit of trouble approaching others to demonstrate his kindness.

In each of these cases, the person's intrinsic nature is not being manifested through his actions, but it nonetheless exists. It is important to recognize that we often do things because of our intrinsic nature, not vice versa. Because I am a kind person, I will often do kind things. I am not a kind person *because* I do kind things; regardless of what I do, I recognize that I am intrinsically kind.

I don't believe that anyone has the capacity to attain the pinnacle of self-esteem. We all have at least vestiges of externally based feelings within ourselves. The goal is to come as close to that pinnacle as possible. Some people want only to build self-esteem so as to reduce or eliminate depressive or anxious feelings. Others view this system as a lifelong goal of moving continually closer to a "perfect" sense of self.

In chapter 1, we mentioned one of the great ironies of self-esteem: the contrast between our ability to feel good about ourselves and our ability to feel good about others. Although most of us have the tendency to view ourselves almost completely based on external factors, we nonetheless are often able to like others on more intrinsic bases.

Consider someone you know well and like. Ask yourself what it is about him that you like and appreciate. The answer often relates to how kind-hearted he is, how interesting he is, or any number of other internally based qualities. We generally don't like people for their accomplishments, their looks, their fashion sense, or other purely external qualities.

The irony lies in the fact that, in reality, the only person whose intrinsic qualities you can truly access is you. Regardless of how well you know someone, you can't possibly be certain of what is going on in his heart and mind. You do, however, know how *you* think and feel. We nevertheless find it so much easier to have "other-esteem" than to have self-esteem. We like others for who they are, though we cannot be certain of their intrinsic nature; yet we have trouble liking ourselves for who we are.

One possible reason for this seemingly converse thought process relates to the very fact that we do not have access to others' thoughts and feelings and we do have access to our own. Since we cannot view others in that way, we are forced, by default, to view them as based on external factors. It is through these external factors that we gain insight into others' intrinsic nature. Since most people are acutely aware of their actions and other external factors, they tend to "put their best foot forward," showing us factors that we will like.

On the other hand, since we are profoundly aware of our own thoughts and feelings, we are in the position to constantly question our actions and the motives for them. Basically, we continuously barrage ourselves with thoughts, both positive and negative, thereby sabotaging our ability to simply feel good about who we are.

On the other side of the coin, however, the relationship between thought and emotion is reciprocal. Therefore, in the same way that our ingrained feelings about ourselves make us believe negative things about ourselves, we can change the way that we feel toward ourselves by changing the way in which we think about ourselves.

Essentially, the identification of intrinsic attributes should be based on thoughts and (more importantly) feelings. With reference to being kind, I can recognize that I am kind because of how I feel toward other people. For instance, I might feel sad when I hear of something bad having befallen someone, or I might feel happy for someone when I hear of their good fortune. Whether or not I act on my feelings is a separate issue that does not speak to who I am.

Sometimes it is difficult to focus on the intrinsic nature of an attribute, and our thoughts keep reverting to actions. In these instances, it can be helpful to consider the reason for the actions. For instance, if the sense is that someone is caring because they do kind things, consider the reason that they do those kind things. What is it that's intrinsic to them that makes them want to do kind things?

Since most of us have been trained since childhood to view ourselves and others through an external lens, we need to retrain ourselves to begin focusing on the internal attributes that we all have.

Another reason that we naturally see others for who they are is that when we reflect on them we view them in a universal sense. We don't ask ourselves what it is about them that we like or respect—we simply feel that way. When we consider ourselves, however, we separate ourselves into many segments, allowing us to incessantly question each one. Basically, while we view others as the sum of their parts, when we view ourselves we focus on the parts.

Learning to view ourselves more universally can help us to begin seeing ourselves as we see others. For some of us, learning to conversely view others in a more compartmentalized fashion can help us to achieve this. The steps described in the next eight paragraphs refer to how we see ourselves. If we wish, we can adapt these concepts to the way in which we view others. This can help us to change our perspective with reference to others in addition to ourselves. Focusing on what we like about someone else's specific *qualities* rather than on the *person* often helps us apply the process to ourselves. Once we learn to appreciate a person's qualities and not simply the person per se, we can start to focus on our own qualities, thereby beginning the process of liking ourselves.

The first step is to identify a number of personal attributes. I often ask people to fill in the blank for the sentence: "I am a _____ person." The one criterion is that the attribute be solely internally based (i.e., not based on actions, surroundings, or what others think or say). Once these attributes are identified, they should be written down in order to work with them.

The next step is to define each attribute, again internally based. For example: Attribute = "kind;" Definition = "feeling for others." This is as opposed to a definition like "always helping others." Another example is: Attribute = "funny;" Definition = "the ability to see humor in life." This would be as opposed to, "makes lots of jokes," or "makes people laugh." The focus is on your thoughts and feelings rather than on your actions.

Being that we are defining these attributes intrinsically and based on emotions and cognition, the specific words that we use to define them need not be in any way similar to a dictionary definition, which may or may not be intrinsically based. In addition, definitions of the same attribute can vary greatly from one person to the next. While one person might define "interest-ing" as "always thinking of odd notions," another person might define it as "enjoyment of diverse thoughts and feelings."

Since personal attributes, for the purpose of self-esteem, should be entirely subjective, what matters is that they be defined intrinsically. In fact, even the desig-nation of the attribute itself is subjective. Use of designa-tions (i.e., "caring" or "loyal") is simply for the purpose of acknowledging and focusing on the thoughts and feelings engendered by them.

To be certain that the attribute is in fact intrinsic and not externally based, there are a couple of scenarios that I will ask you to consider.

The first is to imagine yourself stranded, alone on a deserted island with no hope of ever being rescued. You will never see another person again. There is no need to create shelter or to forage for food. Nothing needs to be done. In this setting, most of the external basis for sense of self disappears. There are no people upon whom to rely for their approval. Possessions, titles, and physical abilities become no longer important. Once this imagery is clear in your mind, ask yourself whether the attribute in question holds true in that situation. If it does, it is likely that it is in fact an intrinsic attribute.

Another scenario, a bit more ethereal, is to imagine yourself as a detached consciousness, or as a soul if you will. In this state, you have no body, none of your five senses, and no ability to do anything other than to think and feel. You exist solely by virtue of your thoughts and emotions. (This can be viewed as the adaptation of "I think; therefore I am" to a state of being). In this state, if properly experienced, nothing external exists at all. While imagining yourself in this state, ask yourself if the attribute applies. If it does, it is highly unlikely that it is externally based.

When imagining either of these scenarios, it is important to envelop yourself within the setting as fully as possible, attempting to "be there" in your mind as completely as possible. The more real the situation appears, the more effectively it will work. Over time, it generally becomes more natural to slip into the scenario and feel a part of it.

Once you have identified and defined your attributes, the real work begins. At this point, you must take time to focus on these attributes, one at a time, placing particular emphasis on their intrinsic nature. Focus is placed on how the particular attribute is manifested in you—what makes you recognize the attribute in yourself, what you admire about the attribute in general, and how you therefore admire yourself for having the attribute.

Although most people tend to focus more on one or two of the attributes than on the others, be sure not to neglect the other, "less important" attributes. Although all of the attributes will be intrinsic, it is nonetheless better to base self-esteem on a more balanced set of attributes.

The more time you give to this exercise, the more quickly you will see results. As time goes on, you will likely find yourself identifying new attributes. As this occurs, the new attributes can be incorporated into your self-definition.

Initially, you will probably find that you begin consciously focusing on these thoughts to combat your old feelings of externally based sense of self. For instance, you might find that you are willing yourself to focus on a particular attribute to help you feel less self-conscious in social situations. As you continue learning to focus on your internal self, however, you will begin recognizing that you are often focusing on this automatically without consciously deciding to. The long-term goal is reached when you are no longer conscious of the thoughts. This will be due to the fact that these thoughts have become feelings and are simply a part of your sense of self. At this point, the external factors that have always affected your sense of self will have a limited ability to do so.

I am often asked whether old, external bases for one's sense of self must be eradicated prior to working on building a new internalized sense of self. I believe that not only is this not necessary, but it can be problematic. Alternatively, I have been asked if an externally based sense of self needs *ever* to be eliminated. In response to these questions, firstly, asking someone to give up a sense of self, however imperfect, is nonetheless asking him to turn his back on who he feels he is. If someone were to accomplish this before building a true sense of self, he might become anxious, depressed, or angry. Secondly, as an intrinsically based sense of self grows stronger, externally based ones continue to grow weaker. Though our sense of self may never be perfectly internalized, its external aspects become continually less pervasive. This can be viewed as a spectrum, one end of which is a completely externalized sense of the world and self, the other end of which is a perfectly internalized sense. Our goal is to continuously strive for the latter.

Incidentally, this concept of a spectrum is very helpful for some people with high anxiety or deep depression who view themselves as different, weird, or abnormal. Recognizing that we are all on the same spectrum but simply in different places on it can help them to feel less like they are in a different sphere of existence from the rest of humanity.

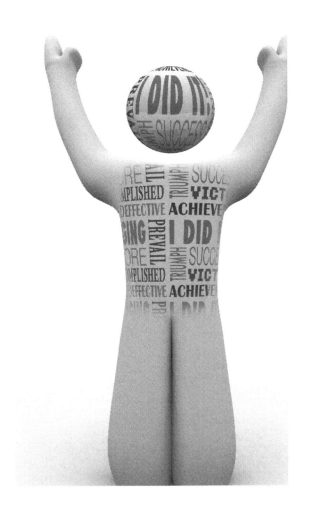

He who controls others may be powerful, but he who has mastered himself is mightier still.
—Lao Tzu

CHAPTER SEVEN
Overcoming Obstacles

Since learning to recognize and to focus on one's intrinsic attributes is an entirely new experience for many of us, there are often obstacles that impede our efforts. Having identified ourselves from early childhood almost exclusively based on externalities, we find ourselves automatically reverting to that way of thinking. Hard as we try to change our perspective, it can be a daunting task.

Many people have trouble simply identifying attributes—they cannot even intellectually recognize their internal qualities. What I often ask people to do in this situation is to think about someone whom they know well. I then ask them to focus on *that* person's attributes. As we mentioned, identifying another person's qualities is often much easier than recognizing our own.

Once another person's attributes are identified and defined (based on the person's intrinsic qualities), they can be applied to the person himself. For instance, we can identify John as a caring person, and define "caring" as "being concerned for others and feeling for them," which is a definition unrelated to external qualities. At that point, the question "Am I a caring person?" is more easily answered. At that point, it is easier to acknowledge the existence of that attribute in ourselves, and to begin focusing on how it feels to have that attribute.

Another method of identifying internal attributes is to try to see yourself from someone else's perspective or through role reversal. Imagining yourself as another person ruminating on *your* qualities can be helpful in identifying your own attributes. In other words, imagine being the other person thinking about you. Be careful, though, to always focus on the person's (i.e., your) internal qualities to avoid falling into the old process of focusing on your actions or externally expressed traits.

In a similar vein, the empty-chair technique can be used. In this scenario, you place a chair a few feet from yourself and imagine yourself sitting in it. You then begin a "conversation" with yourself, asking questions about your internal attributes. Some people find it helpful to have this type of conversation about their qualities, finding that it prompts insightful responses.

Another helpful technique is to keep a journal. Committing your thoughts and feelings to paper often helps you gain a better perspective on your internal attributes. In addition, this can help you remember previous thoughts and to pick up where you left off.

It is important to note that there are people who have been so thoroughly indoctrinated into the notion that external qualities are what make a person who he is that they have trouble identifying intrinsic attributes even in other people. These people do not recognize that there is more to a person than their actions and other external traits. Before working on identifying their personal attributes, these people must first intellectually accept this concept.

Use of the desert island imagery or the concept of detached consciousness, as discussed in chapter 6, can be helpful in beginning to recognize the existence and significance of internal attributes. When a person truly imagines himself, or others, in one of these scenarios, it becomes harder to deny the existence and importance of his intrinsic qualities.

For some, imagining themselves on a desert island can be difficult. Sometimes this is due to lack of imagination. Often, however, this is due to the fact that the very imagery forces people to focus on the reality of who they are. Even recognizing that this is, in fact, the goal of the exercise, they are so entrenched in external validation that this scenario challenges their way of thinking and therefore their (externalized) sense of self. Thus, they shy away from this intellectual challenge even as they recognize its validity.

In some cases, therefore, it may be necessary to begin with more realistic scenarios. These can include family vacation destinations or other places where the person can be alone with his thoughts. It is important, though, to remember that the more realistic and familiar the scenario is, the more likely one is to fall back into old patterns of thinking. It is of utmost importance to clearly focus on the intrinsic nature of the attribute being worked on.

An issue that sometimes arises is that the person feels he needs to be the epitome of a particular attribute in order for him to acknowledge it as an intrinsic quality of himself. For instance, "If I don't always feel caring, I can't recognize myself as a caring person." Or, "Since I'm not the funniest person I know, I can't view myself as a funny person."

The irony of our egocentrism once again becomes clear: though we each individually tend to view the universe as revolving around ourselves, when we view ourselves we focus on specifics, not on an overall sense of who we are. When we view others, however, most of us can see them simply for who they generally are. Therein lies the solution to this obstacle. If we can recognize that we view ourselves very differently than we view others, we can begin to consciously apply that way of thinking to ourselves.

It can also be helpful to understand the reason that most of us are naturally able to recognize others' attributes in this broad fashion. Although altruism versus egoism has been debated by philosophers for many centuries, the basis for the debate has mostly been human behavior and the way in which it is understood. Recognition and exploration of the thoughts and feelings behind the actions are usually absent from the debates. Since the way in which we view ourselves is of utmost importance to us, we apply the prevalent logic to our feelings about ourselves. Our view of others, though, need not be viewed through this prism since it does not take on the same importance for us.

Another obstacle that can crop up in our efforts to become intrinsically self-aware relates to the fact that we have been trained to view the world through an external lens. Even once we recognize the veracity of an internalized sense of self, we can easily revert to old patterns of thought. We sometimes find ourselves reliving past experiences and having feelings similar to those that we've had at those times.

Even when we do not acknowledge particular memories, we often experience emotions that are clearly reactions to childhood experiences. In these instances, we often feel like we did as children, for instance wanting to cry or to throw a tantrum.

Rather than fighting these thoughts, the solution is often to encourage these memories, but to separate physical experience from the feelings associated with them. If, for instance, a particular incident made you feel like an idiot, allow yourself to recall and relive the event and analyze the resultant emotions. Then focus on how a similar incident occurring today might be experienced differently. This can help in two ways. Firstly, it reinforces a general internalized sense of self. Secondly, it can help to change the feelings associated with the original event, thereby decreasing the likelihood of it being triggered in the future.

There are people who find that acknowledging their intrinsic attributes makes them feel uncomfortable. Sometimes it initially even makes them feel worse about themselves. I have identified three possible reasons for this. Some people feel simply that they are aspiring to an unreachable goal; once they clearly recognize the extent to which their sense of self is externally based, they feel overwhelmed by the task at hand.

What I tell these people is to focus on two factors. The first is the fact that no one has the capacity to fully reach the goal of perfect self-esteem. Absolute, perfect self-esteem is only a theoretical goal. Our true goal is to move closer to that theoretical goal. When viewed as a spectrum, it is often easier for people to begin working on slowly changing their sense of self.

The second factor is that the focus should be on interim goals rather than on the ultimate goal. An initial goal might be to recognize a certain number of self-attributes when consciously contemplating them. The second goal might be to be generally aware of these attributes even when not making a conscious effort to ponder them. The next goal could be to feel a positive sense about these attributes, then to feel good about yourself when recognizing these attributes in yourself… As long as there are specified interim goals, the sense of being overwhelmed is mitigated.

Another reason that people might feel worse when contemplating their personal attributes is that they have built an externalized sense of self based on external factors. Considering intrinsic attributes threatens the survival of the only sense of self that they have known.

In this scenario, the focus needs to be on the fact that we are not attempting to relinquish an old sense of self. Rather, we are simply attempting to develop a new one. With time, our reliance on the old, imperfect one will diminish, but that is not our aim; our aim is to learn to focus on the new one. The old sense of self need not be relinquished until we are ready to give it up, which will likely be in stages, rather than in one fell swoop.

Another reason that people can feel badly within the process of considering sense of self is that they fear that in seeking their positive attributes, they might discover that they do not possess any.

It is essential to recognize that we all possess positive attributes. In fact, if a particular attribute is important to us, once it is defined completely intrinsically, it is almost inevitable that we *do* possess it. When someone ascertains that he does not have an intrinsic attribute that he values, this is usually because it hasn't been properly defined. The reason for this is that if you like people who are caring (as based on your definition), you must be a caring person. Otherwise why would this be important for you? Why would a person like others for their caring *nature* if he did not feel this way himself?

It is important to recognize any obstacles that impede our ability to work on our sense of self. Acknowledging these obstacles is the first, crucial step in beginning to eliminate them. As a true, intrinsic sense of self is continuously worked on and developed, these obstacles tend to crop up less often and less strongly. Generally this also means that as one's sense of self grows, obstacles diminish.

It can be helpful to document our progress to prevent us from becoming frustrated at a perceived lack of progress. We tend to view ourselves as unchanging. Though we can see change in others, it can be difficult to recognize progress in ourselves. By documenting a baseline, and acknowledging progress from that starting point, we can alleviate much of the frustration that might otherwise impact us. This will, in turn, give us continued incentive to carry on.

As more people utilize these concepts to build true self-esteem, the potential exists to completely, positively transform social interactions and the way in which both life and happiness are understood.

ABOUT THE AUTHOR

Yehuda Lieberman is a practicing psychotherapist in New York. He has published articles in the Jewish Press and on various mental health websites. He graduated *summa cum laude* with a Bachelor's degree in Psychology from Touro College in New York in 1995 and received the psychology award at graduation. He graduated with an MSW from Yeshiva University's Wurzweiler School of Social Work in New York in 1997. Upon graduation, he worked as a psychotherapist in both clinic and practice settings. In 2001, he began his private psychotherapy practice in New York. He lives in New York with his wife and four children.

REFERENCES

American Psychiatric Association: *Diagnostic and Statistical Manual of Mental Disorders*, Fourth Edition, Text Revision. Washington, DC, American Psychiatric Association, 2000.

Erikson, E. H. (1950). *Childhood and society.* New York: Norton.

Maslow, A.H. (1943). A Theory of Human Motivation. *Psychological Review, 50(4),* 370-396.

Maslow, A.H. (1949). The Expressive Component of Behavior. *Psychological Review, 56(5),* 261-272.